Shore Fishing in Aruba

A guide to Aruba's shore fishing locations

Mike Harry

First printing: April 2015
Published by Interactive Hardware.
ISBN: 978-0-9937694-1-2

Shore Fishing in Aruba
by Mike Harry

Contact: www.interactive-hardware.com
admin@interactive-hardware.com

Ordering Information:
Special discounts are available on quantity purchases by corporations, sports clubs, tourism associations and others. For details, contact the publisher at
admin@interactive-hardware.com

This guide book is based solely on the authors personal experiences shore fishing in Aruba. Rights of access and location conditions may change at any time. Please check before venturing out to any of the locations mentioned here. Always take appropriate safety equipment and never take personal risks, or endanger others while out fishing.

Table of Contents

Shore Fishing in Aruba………………………..….… 1

Basic Equipment…………………………………. 3

Aruba Shoreline Fishing Locations ……………..….. 11

California Lighthouse………………………………. 10

Arashi Beach Grass Flats……………………….. 16

Malmok Cliffs……………………………..……. 20

The Antilla Wreck……………………………........ 24

High Rise Hotel Area - Beaches………………… 26

Low Rise Hotel Area - Beaches………………… 28

Oranjestad Harbour – No Fishing……………….. 30

Spanish Lagoon …………………………………. 31

The old road Bridge…………………………… 33

DePalm Island Parking Lot………………...…… 36

Pirata Marina…………………………………… 39

Balashi Gold Mill Ruins…………….....……….. 41

Mangel Halto Mangroves............................. 45

Isla D'Oro Ruins.. 49

Savaneta Mangroves 51

Savaneta Old Jetties.................................... 53

Baby Beach... 55

Rogers Beach.. 57

A walk on the Wild Side – Surf Casting........... 59

Boca Grandi.. 61

Bushiribana smelter ruins............................. 65

Alto Vista Chapel Trail split 69

Rigs, Worms and Cranks 72

Crankbaits 101.. 79

Chum and pack-bait Combo........................... 91

About the Author... 93

Shoreline fishing in Aruba

For an island that is just 20 miles long by 6 miles wide, Aruba offers a surprisingly diverse range of shoreline fishing locations:

- Shallow grass flats

- Mangroves

- Big surf

- Cliffs and reefs

- Lagoons and estuaries

No fishing license is required for shore fishing in Aruba, but be aware that spearfishing is forbidden by law.

Aruba has a very small tidal range, averaging less than 1.5ft. Despite this, the normal expectations about improved shore fishing around the turn of low tide, (especially at night) still apply.

In view of the high water clarity along the shallow side of the island and the high number of bright sunny days, shallow water fishing is normally at its peak at first light and again around sunset.

The exceptions to this generalisation would be fishing the rough surf zones on the north-east coast, the heavy cover of the mangroves of Mangel Halto and the inshore end of Spanish Lagoon. These areas provide considerably more cover for fish and the shadows can be very productive on bright, sunny days.

Basic Equipment

When fishing on vacation you need to streamline your tackle selection. Thankfully, you can still have a very successful fishing trip to Aruba, or a day shore fishing during your family vacation if you plan ahead and choose your equipment carefully.

Although Aruba does not have any of the big box fishing stores that you may enjoy visiting back at home, basic fishing tackle such as hooks, weights and fishing line can be picked up at any of the small hardware stores that are dotted across the island.

Pictured above: A typical Aruban hardware store's fishing section.

The local shore fishing method uses a large bobbin style hand reel (pictured far right, above) and a balloon, so don't expect to find conventional fishing rods in any of the hardware stores.

I have put together a basic list of the fishing related items that I have found to be essential on my adventures around the Aruban coastline. Use my list as a general reference, read the book for location details, and then re-prioritise the list with equipment that you feel you need for your fishing trip.

The first items on the list are not strictly fishing tackle, but are absolutely required if you are fishing in Aruba.

High SPF Sunscreen – Aruba is very close to the equator, so proper steps need to be taken in order to avoid sunburn and heatstroke.

Wide brim Hat – A good quality wide brimmed hat (Tilley for example) will keep the sun off your neck and provide a little shade over your sunglasses.

Polarised Sunglasses – There can be a lot of glare on the water, so be sure to add a pair of polarised sunglasses to your kit list. It helps if you can see the fish in the shallows at least as well as they can see you. If you can find the polarised glasses with colour tinting, I can recommend the warmer orange or gold coloured lenses over the colder blue or dark grey.

Wading shoes – Don't go wading into the shallows around the mangroves or the grass flats without protecting your feet. There are a lot of sharp roots and pieces of dead coral. Avoid open toe sandals and invest in a pair of quick draining, quick drying boat or kayak shoes.

Insect repellent – If you are intent on fishing around the edges of the mangroves, make sure you have a decent insect repellent such as deep woods OFF.

Water bottle – Although Aruba is a small island, it is easy to find yourself a long walk from a store when in need of a cool drink under the strong sun. Pack some bottled water before setting out.

You will need to take your own rods and reels with you on your trip to Aruba, and there are a number of decent travel rods available to choose from at the major fishing stores, or online. If you are looking to pick one up before setting out on your trip, here are a few travels rods that I can personally recommend, having used them successfully on a few of my fishing trips:

The three piece Offshore Angler travel rods available at Bass Pro. The heavy version can deal with most fish up to about 25 lbs. For lure and plug casting the spinning model is a very good and cost effective option.

(Note: Avoid the short Bass Pro brand telescopic rod at all costs.)

The Shimano Exage series of travel rods are extremely well built, and in particular the telescopic Exage spinning rods are worth the extra money. They perform extremely well and are light years ahead of the usual "broom handle" unresponsive, twenty dollar telescopic rods.

The Magnum Baja travel rod series from Rapala have proven to be my most worthwhile investment. They are available in various weights and lengths from 7ft 6 inches, right up to 13ft 6 inches. The rods break down into four sections, making them easy to pack.

I usually pack two of these rods even when taking a small suitcase, a 7ft light-medium for spinning and the 13ft 6 inch heavy model for beach casting.

Reels – I normally pack two spinning reels with an extra line spool for each. A standard 4000 series, medium sized spinning reel loaded with 10lb hybrid line, and a spool of 12lb mono. The second reel is my monster 7000 series size spinning reel and two spools packed with as much 30lb braid as I can fit onto them.

Plastic storage boxes - I try to keep the bulk of my tackle down to a maximum of four plastic storage boxes. I prefer the type with multiple latches for locking down the lid.

- One box of weights, split shot, swivels, hooks

- One box of assorted crankbaits

- One box of top-water plugs and light spinners

- One box of assorted plastics and streamers etc.

A spare spool of fishing line - Useful for making up new rigs and traces while you are fishing, or replacing leaders without stripping line from your reel.

Steel leaders – A pack or two of Steel leaders will go a long way if you intend to fish the Surf side of the Island.

Bait bag - A small, washable, foil lined, zip up bait bag designed for carrying packs of bait.

Multi-pocket backpack - A backpack with as many pockets on the outside as you can find, but small enough to either fit into the top of your case, or that can double as your cabin bag on the plane (without the fishing tackle in it).

The species that you are likely to encounter in Aruba could mean having to deal with a hook set behind rows of sharp teeth, or handling a fish armed with razor sharp fin spines. You should plan ahead and pack a small fishing related toolkit for these situations.

- A small multi-tool (such as a Leatherman.)

- A long pair of long nose pliers for deep hooks.

- A small pair of wire cutters for cutting hooks.

- A non-slip glove.

- Two flashlights, one clip on, one handheld.

- A small first aid pack.

- A whistle.

- A hand cloth.

- Cellphone.

Your list could easily have a hundred items if you took it down to the detail level, naming specific types of lures, or itemising "a reel of spider wire" etc. Select your target locations and revise your own personalised list.

Obviously, you don't need to carry multiple rods and reels for a sunset fishing session on the Malmok cliffs. But you would be foolish to head out onto the rock platforms on the surf side of the island for a full day's fishing without drinking water, sun protection, a first aid kit, a cell phone and a whistle.

So plan ahead, check the weather, wind and water conditions, pick your fishing locations for the day or night, and pack accordingly.

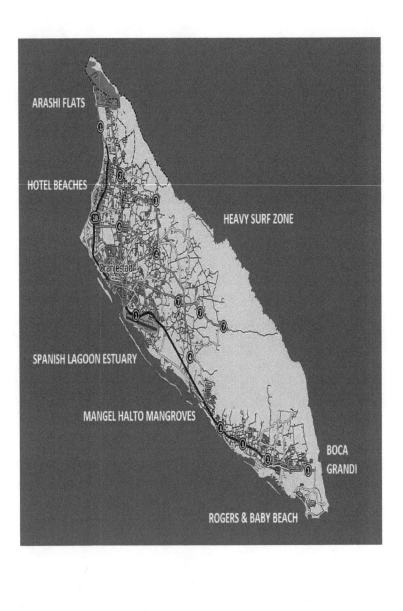

ARASHI FLATS

HOTEL BEACHES

HEAVY SURF ZONE

Oranjestad

SPANISH LAGOON ESTUARY

MANGEL HALTO MANGROVES

BOCA
GRANDI

ROGERS & BABY BEACH

Aruba Shoreline Fishing Locations

Northwest shoreline

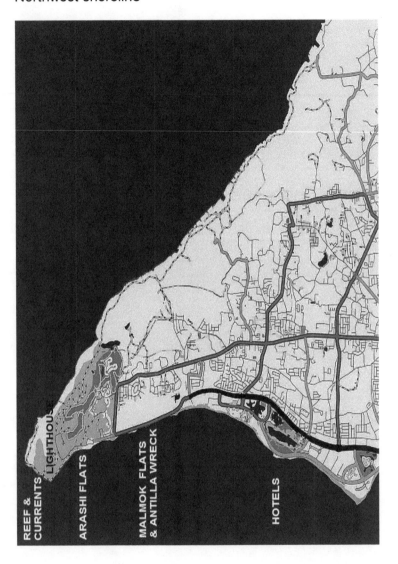

REEF & CURRENTS

LIGHTHOUSE

ARASHI FLATS

MALMOK FLATS & ANTILLA WRECK

HOTELS

California Lighthouse

The northern tip of the island, in front of the California lighthouse is comprised of sharp volcanic rock platforms and coral reefs. The water here is subject to fierce cross rips between the prevailing winds and currents.

Extreme caution should be observed when fishing this area. GPS: 12.619758, -70.058290

Protective footwear is essential. Night fishing alone is not recommended due to the severe nature of the terrain underfoot.

NOTE: On rough weather days it is not advisable to fish here at all. Sudden swells can completely engulf the lower rock platforms and easily sweep you off into the surf.

To access the northern tip dirt road, drive north on the main highway out of Oranjestad beyond the high rise hotels, following the road signs for the California lighthouse. Once you have passed all the houses and are nearing the lighthouse, you will see a pair of stone gateways on the left side of the road. These are the entrance and exit for the Arashi Beach parking lot.

Immediately beyond the second, northern most entrance to the parking lot, there's a dirt road (opposite street pole number 20 if you are checking). This is the path that will lead you around the edge of the rocky coast, onto the rough shore directly in front of the lighthouse. GPS: 12.613259, -70.055134

If you deploy the Aruban balloon fishing method here, or distance cast using cut or live bait, there is a good possibility of landing one of the larger reef predator species at either end of the day. I recommend the use of a steel leader if fishing at sunset when the larger predators move inshore. You can also spend an hour drop shot fishing straight down off the ledges with small hooks and bait particles, in order to catch bait fish for use as live bait. Garfish around four feet in length are a relatively common catch here.

Arashi beach Grass flats

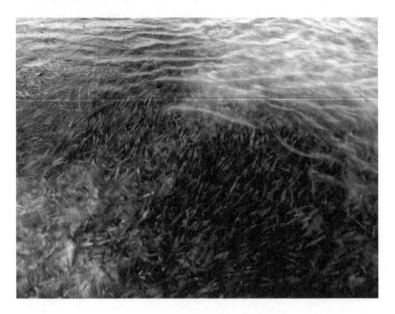

There are several areas of shallow grass flats located around Aruba's western shoreline. The upper, Arashi beach grass flats are situated just below the northwest corner of the island. Follow the driving directions previously detailed for accessing the northern coast dirt road, but turn into the stone walled Arashi Beach parking lot, instead of taking the dirt road further north.

GPS: 12.612758, -70.055358

A complete lack of cover throughout the majority of the day can severely limit the fish traffic across the shallows after sun rise, along with the kite surfers and jet skis roaring about on the surface.

At first light of dawn and again at sunset are the best times to fish the Arashi beach grass flats.

First thing to note - Don't be in a rush to start wading into the water!

Just walk the edge of the water along the beach fan casting and retrieving a pike feather into the shallows. While walking along, look for signs of fish action further out. On several occasions I have taken my first fish of the day in less than a foot of water, just a couple of feet from the beach, long before I have gotten my feet wet wading out onto the grass banks.

When you do see sign of fish action further out, move slowly and quietly into the shallow water and out onto the mounds of sea grass while keeping a look out for fish swirls and those dark, shiny tail fins breaking the surface.

A number of the fish species that hunt across the flats get spooked very easily, so smaller lures and a stealthy approach are the best tactics to deploy. White and silver pike streamer feathers have worked very well for me on several occasions, and the use of a small top water plug can also be effective, if you are patient and pause for a minute or two after the initial splash.

This is a great area for fly fishing techniques, and you can also get good results with light spinning tackle, if you can effectively mimic fly fishing tactics. Targeted long distance casts, stripping large steamers or imitation crayfish.

Watch for the diving Pelicans to indicate where the bait fish are. Slowly wade toward these areas if you can, as the predator species won't be far away.

Expect to encounter a wide number of species depending on the time of year, Garfish, various types of Jacks, Snappers, Trumpet fish, small Snook, Ladyfish and medium sized Bonefish when in season.

Malmok cliffs

The most popular fishing spot on the island, with local families setting up for night time fishing sessions on the stone platforms at sunset. The Aruban shore fishing method involves no conventional fishing rod and spinning reel, relying instead on large bobbin-style hand reels, and drifting live or cut bait out onto the reef, suspended under a party balloon.

If you want to give it a try, you can pick up one of the hand reels at any hardware store on the island. I usually combine the Aruban method with my conventional rod and reel, using the balloon as a wind drifted float to take my bait our over the reef and deep water. Plan ahead and take a pack of bio-degradable latex balloons.

Malmok Cliffs and bays are situated on the main road heading north from the High rise hotels, just as you approach the left fork in the road that leads to Arashi and the road sign for the California lighthouse.

GPS: 12.601356, -70.051037

There's lots of parking space available on the dirt track, right at the junction. You can also choose a quieter location on one of the stone platforms slightly further south down the main road, back towards the high rise hotels.

There a few points to be aware of at this location.

- Local commercial fisherman will be active just offshore right before sunset and again at first light. If you are drifting a balloon, be careful of their lines, nets and boat propeller!

- If you are at the south end of the rock platforms during the late afternoon, you will have to wait for the local party boats to move off at sunset.

- Keep a lookout for groups of snorkelers passing by in the shallows.

- Once the sunset is well underway, this is a busy shore fishing spot. You will need a flashlight or two as there are no streetlights near the water's edge.

While I practice catch and release fishing, many of the families fishing at this location are doing so in order to put fresh fish on the dinner table. I have made many friends and received some excellent tips and even fresh bait, in exchange for offering my catches to nearby family groups.

If you are lucky enough to land a decent catch here, think about generating some good will and a bit of positive karma.

Setting up for a night session of distance casting cut baits from the Malmok cliffs can be very worthwhile. However, you will need to select your location before sunset, as moving around on the platforms after dark can be very dangerous. If you have a distance casting rod, you can set up on the sand in one of the small inlets and have a very comfortable fishing session on your own private mini-beach.

Weights of at least 2oz will be required for distance and holding your bait in position. Use grip leads if you can. Hooked cut baits on the sea bed, in combination with a chum / pack-bait will bring in decent fish.

Read the Chum / pack-bait article on page 91 for details on how to assemble your pack-bait if you are interested in this type of fishing session.

The Antilla wreck

South of the Malmok cliffs and north of the high-rise hotels, the remains of the WW2 Dutch freighter The Antilla sits grounded on a long stretch of shallow water.

The ship was originally sunk offshore in forty feet of water to prevent its capture by German forces in WW2. A popular diving and snorkeling spot for many years, the wreck of The Antilla was lifted from the sea floor during a major storm in 2005 and pushed up the beach onto the shallows.

GPS: 12.591850, -70.047906

As with fishing the north end of the Arashi flats, keep a slow, stealthy approach and make good use of distance casting and stripping streamers and small top water lures through the water.

Sunrise is by far the best time of day for fishing this location. Be prepared to wade out a fair distance and cast as close to the wreck as you can as it provides significant fish cover.

NOTE: Always wear proper foot protection when wading across the shalllows.

High rise Hotel Area - beaches

The beaches in Aruba are public, but the majority of the beach facilities, such as the lounge chairs, sun shades, and piers are privately owned. The long stretch of public beach in front of the high rise hotels can provide excellent overnight and early morning surf fishing.

GPS: 12.574326, -70.044547

The best time to fish this particular stretch of beach and piers in front of the high rise hotels is the early hours of the morning, after the pier bars have closed for the night. Don't try this while the beach and bars are still in full swing. Most of the piers are marked no fishing and have security guards, but you can wade out waist deep into the public waters directly alongside them, and pitch a lure along the shadow line to target fish lurking beneath them.

Once the tourists start to emerge onto the beach after sunrise there will be too much noise and traffic, both in the water and on the surface from boats and jet skis etc.

If you are the fishing pre-dawn, you can also walk the shoreline fan casting a small trout spinner, a crankbait or pike feather into the surf.

Beachcasting:

Static night fishing on the hotel beaches can be very productive. Set up a long beach caster down at the water's edge after dark and cast cut bait with a chum / pack-bait combo.

See the Chum / Pack-bait article on page 91 for details.

Low rise Hotel Area – beaches

Just north of Oranjestad, located along the shoreline near the original low rise hotels area, there are a series of long stone breakwaters extending out from the beaches. The area is signposted as the low rise hotels, and there is off road parking just south of the hotel stretch, right next to the start of the beaches.

GPS: 12.561702, -70.054005

I can usually manage a longer fishing session in the mornings here than further up the beach at the high rise area. If you are out on the end of the stone breakwaters, you are usually further out than the majority of beachgoers.

Bright coloured spinners and crankbaits deliver excellent results here, when cast along the sides and ends of the breakwaters. There are a lot of Jacks and snappers around the rocks in this stretch of water.

Although it is sometimes possible to fish here throughout the day and evening, keep a watch out for jet skis and snorkelers.

Oranjestad harbour where the charter boats are located is privately owned and posted as a no fishing zone.

Spanish Lagoon.

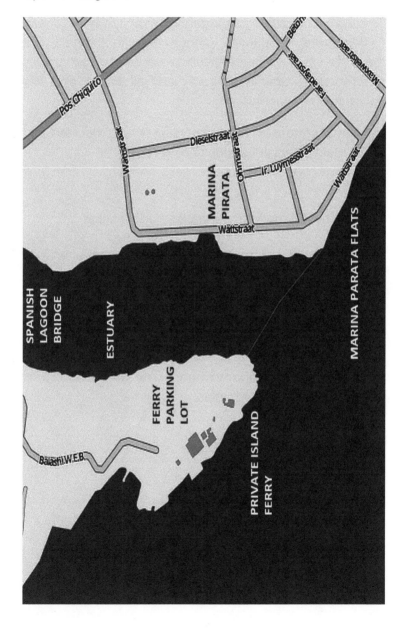

Spanish Lagoon.

There's a lot of confusion regarding exactly where to start fishing around "Spanish Lagoon" due to the fact that there are several different fishing locations, all generically referred to as Spanish Lagoon, and all worthy of a few hours of trying your luck.

In attempting to clarify the confusion, I have detailed four of the main Spanish Lagoon fishing spots:

- The old road bridge, pedestrian crossing.

- The estuary shoreline cliffs on the north side, next to the De Palm island ferry terminal parking lot.

- The estuary shoreline and shallow flats on the south side, at Marina Pirata.

- The inland lagoon mangroves and shallows at Balashi Gold mill ruins.

Spanish Lagoon - The old road bridge

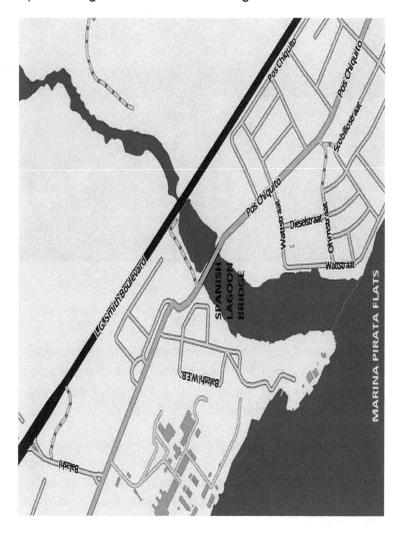

Spanish Lagoon – old road bridge

There are two road bridges crossing the Spanish Lagoon estuary. The main highway bridge from Oranjestad to San Nicholas (not fishable) and the old road bridge situated further downstream.

There is also what looks like a large third "bridge" of sorts even further downstream in the estuary from the road bridges, but this is in fact an elevated pipeline crossing, not fishable and just adds to the bridge location confusion.

GPS: 12.473245, -69.974965

To Access the old road bridge and its pedestrian walkway, you need to take the main road south from Oranjestad, head past the airport until you reach the traffic light junction next to the enormous blue and white Balashi Beer brewery on your right.

Take the right turn off the main highway at the Balashi Brewery traffic lights, then turn left at the bottom of the side street. Follow the road straight on down the hill and across the old road bridge. There is parking space off the road at the south end of the bridge. The pedestrian walkway is easily accessed from the parking spot.

Be aware that this is a busy, narrow road and do not sit on the bridge wall or stand in the traffic lane on the bridge. Take extra caution whenever you position your fishing rod overhead, always check that there is no road traffic, or better still learn to side cast before you go.

It is possible to climb down off the walkway into the shallow water in front of the bridge if you are equipped for wading, but this is not really required to effectively fish this location, and the water becomes very deep just a few feet from the bridge. You can expect a wide range of species here including Jack and juvenile Barracudas, depending on the time of day or night and the style of fishing you undertake. Once the sun is up over your shoulder, you should transfer you attention to casting towards the overhanging mangroves along the southern shoreline extending downriver from the bridge. Careful pitching of top water lures and small spinners or plastics will attract the attention of the many fish hiding among the roots and branches.

DePalm island ferry - parking lot

The DePalm Island parking lot is situated on the north shore of the Spanish Lagoon estuary. To get there, travel south from Oranjestad on the main road past the airport. Take the Balashi Brewery turn off on your right, then turn left onto the old road at the bottom of the brewery side road. Follow the DePalm Island road signs and turn right, off the old road, before you reach the Spanish Lagoon old road bridge. GPS: 12.471635, -69.977259

Take the side road down through the old housing estate until you sweep right at the end of the street into the ferry parking lot. Head diagonally to your left across the empty yard – parking lot and you will spot a trail opening in the bushes to the left side of the Aruba boat club marina.

Take a short walk through the bush trail and you will emerge on the cliffs, across the estuary from Marina Pirata.

The cliffs slope downward significantly lower to the water the further you head out along the estuary. From the lowest corner of the cliffs you can easily cast out onto the open shallows between Spanish Lagoon and the private island.

Be very cautious about fishing here after dark, there are numerous gaps and ravines in the cliffs.

Marina Pirata – View from the cliffs at DePalm Island ferry parking lot.

Pirata Marina - South shore of the Spanish Lagoon estuary.

To access the shoreline on the south side of the Spanish Lagoon estuary, take the Balashi Beer brewery turn off on the main road. Turn left at the bottom off the hill and head straight on past the Depalm Island side street, drive across the Spanish Lagoon old road bridge, and take the next paved road on the right. GPS: 12.468992, -69.975489

Follow the signs for Marina Pirata to the end of the street, drive around the corner past the restaurant until you come to the stone platforms and shallow flats on your right.

This is a great wading spot and fly, streamer or spin casting location.

Be aware that it is very popular with locals as a swimming spot throughout the day and early evening, and there are usually a few local fishermen deploying balloon rigs onto the estuary at night.

Evenings and overnight fishing, distance casting or balloon drifting live or cut bait out onto the lagoon will put you onto predator fish moving in and out of the Estuary.

Balashi Gold Mill - The Spanish Lagoon Mangroves.

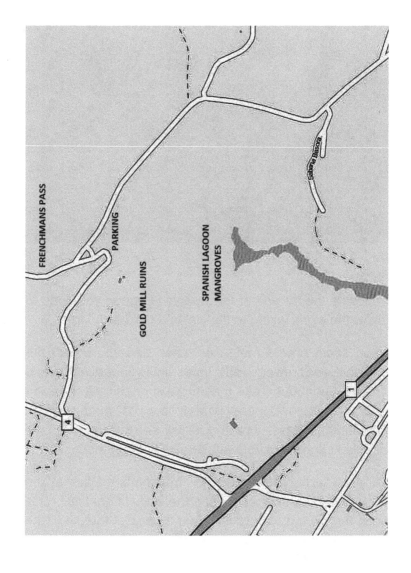

To locate the far end of the Spanish Lagoon you need to follow the signs inland to the Balashi Gold Mill ruins.

Head south on the main road past the airport, past the Balashi Beer brewery traffic lights until you reach the next major roundabout. Take the third exit on the left, heading inland (Sabana Basora) and follow the road towards Frenchmans Pass, where you will see the shoreline of Spanish Lagoon on your left side as you approach.

As you reach the entrance to Frenchmans Pass at the base of the valley, you will see the Balashi gold mill ruins upon the hill top to your left. At the base of the dip in the road, take the left exit and make a U-turn onto the gold mill road. GPS: 12.483663, -69.971533

On the approach road to the ruins, turn off into the dirt parking lot and walk through the stones barrier to the water.

To fish effectively here, you need to be equipped for wading.

Be sure to pack bug spray as the Mangroves are home to a multitude of biting insects. Protective footwear is essential when wading here.

Trout spinners, small plastics and pike streamers are effective lures for targeting the fish among the roots and shallows.

Mangel Halto Mangroves

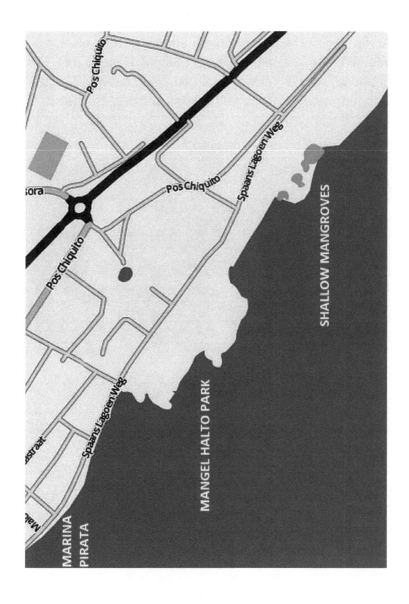

The old shoreline road past Marina Pirata will lead you a short distance south east to the start of Aruba's Mangrove coast.

At the end of the Marina Pirata stretch of rock platforms, you will see the entrance to Mangel Halto park. The entrance path is clearly marked, just head down the wooden walkway, through the trees and onto the beach.

GPS: 12.465181, -69.969692

The shallow flats at Mangel Halto can be waded for quite some distance heading south east along the coast.

Unlike the open flats further up along the northwest coast, the mangroves provide significant fish cover during the day. So while there may be higher fish traffic at first and last light, there is still a decent chance of drawing a fish out from the edges of mangrove cover throughout the day. Wade out as far as you can and cast back toward the edge of the forest. Keep an eye on the stone lines in the shallows, running parallel to the beach. This is a great location for spotting predator fish on the prowl in the early mornings.

Isla D'Oro ruins

If you follow the pipeline along the edge of the road southbound from Mangel Halto towards Savaneta, you will come across the Isla D'Oro ruins on your right just as the pipeline road swings left to rejoin the main road. At the time of writing (2015) it was still possible to easily access the mangrove pathway from the road entrance through to the lagoon and reef top buildings beyond.

Take extreme care as the pathway was showing signs of collapse as of 2015. If the pathway is no longer open or safe to walk on, you can still access the lagoon, reef and ruined buildings by simply wading along the shallows on the outside of the Savaneta mangroves.

GPS: 12.458579, -69.959925

Savaneta Mangroves

Follow the pipeline road south again beyond Isla D'Oro until you reach the raised concrete platform crossing the pipelines. This will lead you into the beach and Savaneta's shallow flats area, from where you can wade through the shallows along the edge of the mangrove shoreline. GPS: 12.450863, -69.953295

Isla D'Oro Ruins

Savaneta old Jetties

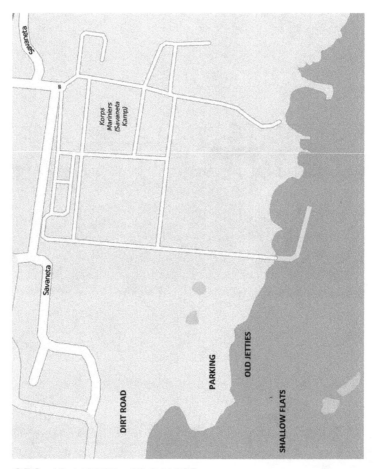

GPS: 12.442887, -69.941020

The final stop on the mangrove section is at the south end of the pipeline road that we have been following all the way down from Marina Pirata. At the point where the road takes a sharp left turn, you can see a set of ruined buildings on the far side of the pipelines to your right.

There's a set of old jetties providing excellent sight lines
and raised casting platforms

The road to Seroe Colorado – Baby Beach

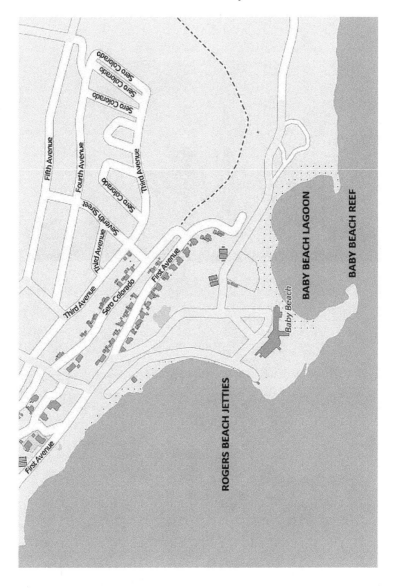

Beyond the town of San Nicholas at the south east point of Aruba, are the lagoons of Baby Beach and Rogers beach. At the time of writing (2015) there are significant repair work and upgrades taking place at the Baby Beach lagoon, with large piles of dead coral lining the outer breakwalls.

A popular beach area, the construction work and significant piles of dead coral do not currently (2015) offer a good fishing location, other than surf casting on the outside of the lagoon. GPS: 12.414658, -69.881667

Along side Baby Beach, towards the oil refinery side, is the bay and dock of Rogers Beach. I have fished here in the early evenings after the local boat fisherman have returned for the day. There are a number of Pelicans that also fish here in the early evenings, so keep a sharp eye on your bait. GPS: 12.415026, -69.884130

You can wade into the shallows alongside the reef edge where Rogers Bay opens onto the sea. Any significant fish traffic into Rogers Bay will pass through this opening.

A Walk on the Wild Side

Surf casting the rough waters of Aruba's eastern shores

This stretch of coastline on Aruba's North-East is a high wind, high surf location. You must have proper footwear, hat and sunscreen. It is possible to reach a number of these coastline locations by mountain bike, but the majority of trips I have made with a day's fishing gear in tow have been by car.

The rough surf side of the island requires distance casting with weight and pack-baits. If you don't have a telescopic rod tripod, I recommend a trip to one of the local hardware stores to buy the parts needed to build your own homemade rod support. I used an inverted wire clothes hanger mounted onto three lengths of pipe, secured with generous amounts of duct tape. I was able to keep my 15ft beachcaster propped at a high angle, despite the constant trade winds.

Large cut baits or squid from the fish freezer at the supermarket, in combination with an oats / fish pack-bait work really well in the surf areas.

A squid fishing trick that I picked up while sea fishing in the UK many years ago is also a great fit for this location:

Slide a small clear plastic bubble float up your line from the hook and inside the squid's body tube. Then slide the float and squid back down the line to the top of your treble hook. This rig allows the squid to "bobble" around over the seabed, giving much more attractive bait movement, and usually results in a more aggressive strike.

You will need heavier weights than usual to hold position, at least 2oz and up. If you don't have spiked, grip weights for sea fishing, make a few homemade ones by adding some opened out paper clips and strong elastic bands to your existing bomb weights. You want the weight to be able to hold position, but also break free when you strike a fish.

Be warned that there are BIG fish in these waters, including reef sharks. You will need the weight correct rod, reel and line for this style of fishing.

Boca Grandi

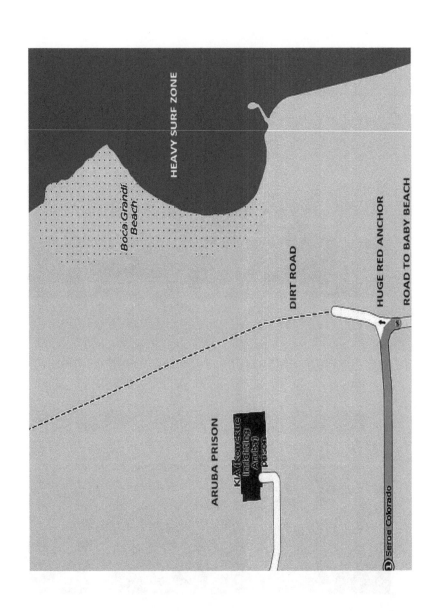

Situated in front of the Aruba prison is Bachelors Beach and Boca Grandi, both excellent surf casting, fishing locations. GPS: 12.437451, -69.876559

To reach it head south through San Nicholas following the signs towards Seroe Colorado and Baby Beach. Before you turn into the Seroe Colorado colony area, you will see the huge Red anchor at a sharp turn in the road. Baby Beach is off to the right, through Seroe Colorado, and Bachelors Beach and Boca Grandi are down the dirt road on the left.

Distance casting beyond the breakers will put your bait into the fish traffic areas. I have taken Jacks and small Barracudas at this location.

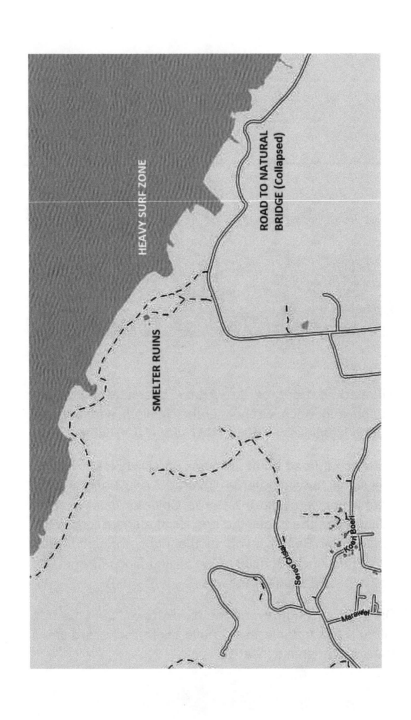

Bushiribana Gold Smelter Ruins

Bushiribana Gold Smelter ruins are located on the eastern shore, north of the national park area and marks the start of a long northward stretch of cliffs and inlets on this rough surf side of the island. Many of the small inlets along this stretch are deserted throughout the day, except for the occasional tourist jeep tour hurtling past at breakneck speed.

Most week days there's a food truck parked at the smelter ruins location, so it's a good spot to take a break between fishing different inlets, find a cold drink and a bite to eat. GPS: 12.553778, -69.976308

To reach the Bushiribana gold smelter ruins follow the road signs for the Natural Bridge (collapsed 2005) and when you reach the large natural bridge board sign, (pictured above) turn left instead of right. You will see the smelter ruins in the distance along the dirt track.

Unlike the shallow beach areas on the western side of the island, these rough water areas can be effectively fished throughout the day.

There are reef sharks and barracudas here, so be prepared. Steel leaders, tough line and breakaway weights are just some of the more specialised equipment you may want to bring, or pick up at the hardware store if you are thinking of making a serious go of surf casting on Aruba's wild side.

The Alto Vista Chapel off road trail split

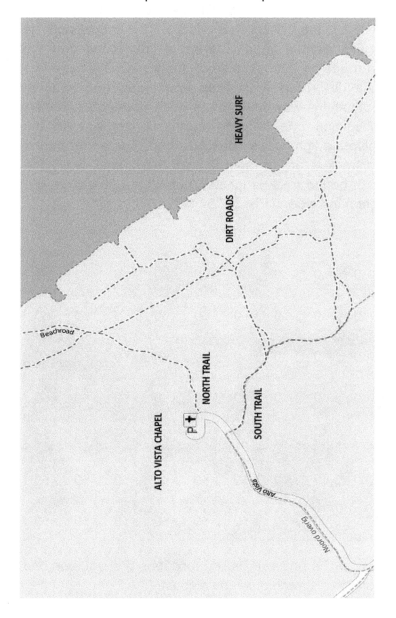

The Alto Vista Chapel is located on a hill above the town of Noord, north of Oranjestad. Follow the road signs for the chapel from Noord. The chapel acts as an important marker in terms of linking together the dirt roads on the east side of the island. There are two main dirt roads accessible from here, one heading south all the way down to the Bushiribana gold smelter ruins, and one heading north all the way to the California lighthouse coastline road. The south bound dirt track is on the approach to the chapel, while the north bound track is located behind the chapel on the right hand side. GPS: 12.574977, -70.011445

Typical cliff and surf fishing locations that you can find along this stretch of Aruba's coast.

SOUTH BOUND DIRT ROAD
ON APPROACH TO CHAPEL

NORTH BOUND DIRT ROAD
BEHIND CHAPEL

Rigs, worms and Cranks

It's worth understanding some of the more popular variations of presentations using plastic worms.

I have listed the more common rigs that I have used in the mangroves and shallows.

Texas Rigged Worm.

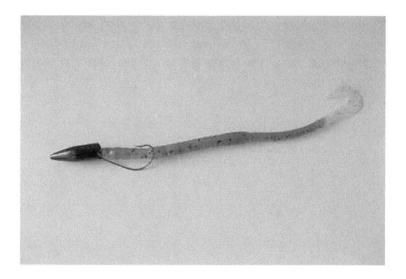

Thread a worm hook through the tip of the worm and twist the hook around, back into the worm, piercing the hook through the body.

The Texas rig is considered the go-to setup for fishing plastic worm lures.

The weight in front of the hook is usually free running on the line. You can skip the lure across the bottom using a vertical twitch and release on retrieve. This will give the worm a nice injured up and down motion, with good variation in speed as the weight slides away from it on the drop and back to it on the upward retrieve. A small bead between the hook knot and the weight will add some sound when the bead and weight collide, and will also protect the knot from wear.

Generally, I only use this set up if the fish are actively biting. I'll switch to a slower presentation, such as a shaky head, or slack lining set up if the fish are being slow and lazy.

The Carolina Rig

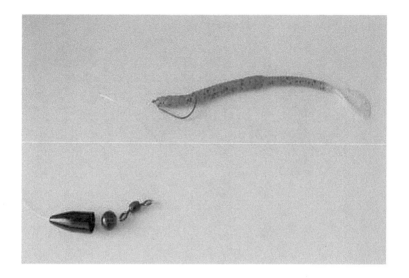

The main difference between a Carolina rig and a Texas rig is that on the Carolina rig the weight is usually set around 1 to 2ft in front of the hook on the other side of a swivel. The section of line between the weight and the worm allows the lure a wider range of free movement, during the drop and retrieve process.

The Carolina rig provides a number of options in presentations and their retrieving speeds. You can use the same vertical twitch and drop motion as with a Texas rigged worm, or you can slowly drag the weight across the bottom. If you are using a floating worm, the lure will stay swimming just above the bed.

Wacky Rigged Worm

A wacky rigged worm is probably the simplest form of worm rig you will find. It's a drop rig, not designed to be drawn or played across the bottom in any way. This presentation is intended to be hit by fish on the slow fall before reaching bottom. Thicker, soft worms tend to perform best, the Senko worm is the go-to worm for most wacky rigs. The idea is for the worm to present a natural, undulating descent in front of the fish. You can use this for great results when plunking in roots or weeds beds, especially when fishing beneath overhanging tree cover.

If you are pitching and retrieving these worms some distance into heavy weeds, the hook can start to tear them up after a few casts. It is common practice to use a small piece of electrical tape or rubber tubing slipped over the worm and pierced by the hook, to give additional support.

Note: Ironically, trying to pull out the hook before you remove your protective tape or tubing will ensure that the hook barb does tear your worm up, so take the tape off first, before trying to replace the worm.

Shaky Head Rig

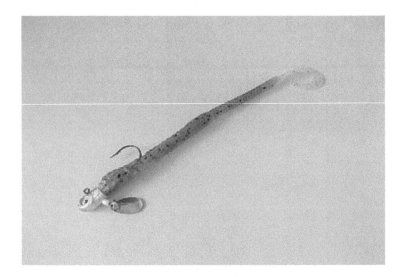

The shaky head rig is an excellent set up for slow days. This set up works best when slowly dragged and twitched across the bottom, or in combination with the slack lining technique. The shaky head rig is designed to be used with a floating worm, so that the tail sticks up and wiggles in the water. I use a horse head jig, as the additional blade really kicks up the sand under the lure.

I prefer to use this presentation when fishing a sand or mud bottomed area. Not suitable for use among heavy weeds.

Crankbaits 101

As crankbaits are so effective in catching so many of the species, I thought that a quick review on the basics of crankbaits, and how to tell a shallow running crank lip from a deep diver might be useful.

The first thing to get out of the way when discussing crankbaits is the lipless crankbait. Lipless cranks are mostly* sinking lures, unlike the various lipped crankbaits which are mostly* floating or neutral buoyancy, and use the lip in order to dive.

Yes there are many exceptions to this generalisation, some of which we will look at, but for the purpose of understanding the basics we will be applying this over-simplified generalization.

Lipless crankbaits use their flat-sided body design and the high position of the top-mounted line tie to produce a narrow swimming action.

Lipless Crankbait

I think it's worth pointing out that the swimming action of the lipless crankbait is intentionally designed as a far more subtle vibrating action, than the typical wide wobble action of a lipped crankbait. So, don't throw out those lipless cranks because they appear to have no action, they're actually working just fine.

The tight vibrating action of a good quality lipless crankbait produces high-frequency vibrations that mimic a wounded baitfish. Generally speaking, because a lipless crank doesn't have the drag caused by a diving lip it is possible to retrieve it at extremely fast speeds, and the faster you retrieve the more intense the vibrations. On the flip side, lipless cranks tend to be poor performers at very slow speeds, especially when compared to a jointed, lipped crankbait.

Lipless, sinking crankbaits will immediately drop through the water column when you cast them out, making these lures useful for targeting fish that are suspended mid or deep water. They generally drop at a rate of a foot a second, allowing you to count them down to a specific depth. The expensive ones come with the sink rate printed on the box. There are a few factors however, that can alter the sink rate, such as your fishing line and water currents. It's always worth applying your own '1 Mississippi, 2 Mississippi' sink rate count test on any new lipless cranks, so you know how fast the crank sinks, at your normal rate of counting.

The length and angle of a crankbait lip determines if it's a deep, shallow, or medium diver. The width of the lip blade compared to the width of the main body, determines the side to side motion....That's it, the end. OK. Not really the end, but understanding how the lip effects action, doesn't have to be any more complicated than that.

The majority of today's mass produced crankbaits contain air chambers that house small metal Ball Bearings. These Ball Bearings emit sound and vibrations when the crankbait moves through the water, which hopefully alerts any nearby predator fish. Without getting overly technical, the size and position of the hollow chamber dictates the buoyancy of the crankbait and determines whether it's a surface floater or suspends in the water when you stop retrieving.

Crankbaits labeled as floating will slowly rise to the surface if you stop retrieving them. When you restart the retrieve, the crankbait will dive according to the angle of the lip. Floating crankbaits are usually the best choice for fishing shallow waters, or water that has heavy weed growth. Floating crankbaits tend to move forward with a head down angle. This puts the lip out front and protects the belly hook behind it. These lures also have a tendency to float up backwards, useful for backing it up from obstacles when you pause the retrieve, or relax the line.

Suspending baits will float on the surface, dive down on the retrieve but will hover and maintain a constant depth when the reeling of the line is halted. This style of bait is great for targeting fish that follow and attack on the pause, or for fish that hunt at a specific depth.

Longer, narrower lips that are connected straight out forward from the nose of the crankbait will dive the deepest, and have the tightest side to side motion. Wide lips that are connected at 60 to 90 degrees down from the front of the crankbait will run shallowest, and have a wide side motion. Lips that are positioned at 30 to 45 degrees will have medium wiggle and medium diving depth.

Shallow running crankbait

A shallow diving crankbait possesses the smallest lip and the steepest angle. It will generally dive less than 5 feet and is used for very shallow water or skimming over the tops of tall weeds.

Medium running crankbait

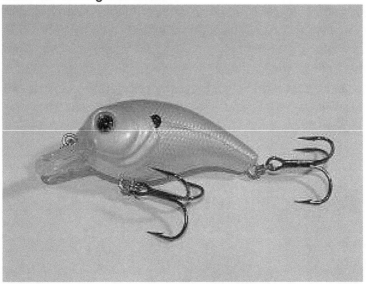

The medium diver has a slightly larger, narrower lip at an angle of around 30 to 45 degrees and can run at depths between 5 and 12 feet.

Deep running crankbait

A deep diving lure has a large lip positioned at a flat angle; some lips are almost as long as the lure body. These deep runners can go down more than twenty feet.

The position of the connection point between the line and the crankbait affects a crankbait's action and diving depth. Take a second look at the shallow running crankbait picture, and you will see that the line connection point is not even on the lip, it's on the front of the head. Now take a second look at the deep running crankbait picture. The line tie on point is halfway down the lip.

It's common practice when buying cheap, mass produced cranks to upgrade the rings and hooks. If you go this route, keep in mind that the hook size directly affects the crankbaits motion and buoyancy. The hooks act in a similar manner to a boat keel by providing downward stability to the lure. Generally speaking, larger hooks offer more stability. However, if the hook is too large, it will also be too heavy, and negatively affect the lure's action, by transforming from keel to anchor. Ideally you want a hook just large enough to provide stability and cleanly hook into your target fish, but small enough to minimize any anchor effect.

The effect of the hook's weight on the lure increases as the distance between it and the line tie increases, meaning that hooks at the rear of the bait will have a greater effect on the lure's swimming action than hooks at the front. Be wary of swapping out a rear treble for a large single hook that has an offset to its curve as this can cause the crankbait to no longer run true in the water.

If you want to change your hook, go ahead, but be prepared to go out and experiment with the modified crankbait in clear water, so you can see what unintentional action changes you may have made.

Exceptions to my scandalous floaters and sinkers generalization....

Minnow Crankbait

The minnow crankbait has undergone significant development in recent years, and you can now find a minnow style crankbait of whatever performance type you require. They can be cranked, popped, trolled, fished top-water as floaters, or paused mid-water at a depth of your choosing.

The Minnow crank typically has a long slender profile, a small shallow diving lip, and slow keel side to side rolling action. At one time the diving lip was always a shallow diving lip, but recently manufacturers have begun offering deeper running models. The longer, slim profile doesn't offer the belly hook protection you get from a head down wide body crank, so you need to keep more of an eye out for snagging. Many manufacturers now also offer floating, slow-rising, and suspending versions.

The suspending models perform in a similar fashion to suspended wide body cranks, resting at a specific depth and allowing you to pause and 'hover" the crank directly over fish holding cover.

The jointed crankbait consists of two or more hinged body segments that create an exaggerated wiggle, even at slow retrieval speeds, giving the appearance of an erratic moving bait fish, unable to gain speed.

Most of the time I tend to favour a jointed body crankbait over the straight body types. I think the jointed crankbait has features that are giving me some additional advantages, namely more movement and vibration noise at much slower retrieval speeds when compared to the single piece crankbaits. A jointed crankbait with good wiggle motion will give both decent rattle and flash as it moves along, even at a dead slow speed.

When I rig a jointed crankbait I prefer to use a wide loop knot on the front and ensure that the crankbait is completely free on the loop to give the maximum side to side motion that it has to offer. Very little forward movement is then required to get a decent side to side wobble going.

Because jointed crankbaits wobble so well even at slow speed retrieval they look like they're trying to move quickly away, but just can't. Perfect for fooling your target into thinking that your lure is an easy meal, an injured baitfish trying to move out of range, and enticing a strike and hook up. I can't overstress the importance of getting a decent jointed crankbait for hi-movement, slow speed retrieval work.

Chum and Pack-bait combo

I have adapted the pack-bait technique that I commonly use during my Carp fishing sessions in Toronto into a successful bait and chum presentation for distance casting in Aruba.

When fishing for Carp I use a combination of Sweetcorn on the hook and additional sweetcorn mixed with oatmeal formed into a sticky paste that is pressed tightly into a ball around the weight and cast out. The Oatpack breaks up on the bed of the lake and forms a pile of oats and corn that drifts around the hook bait.

The Aruba version is very similar, except that the corn is removed from the mix and substituted with chopped and mashed fish, mixed into a little oatmeal.

Rig your line with the weight and a hook length hanging below it. Put a piece or two of cut bait onto the hook. You can whip it on with elastic spider thread or even regular cotton thread if the bait is soft and likely to fly off during casting.

Place a handful of cut oats, the porridge breakfast cereal, but not the instant one minute type, into a plastic container and add a handful of chopped and mashed fish. Mix the two together.

Add a SMALL amount of water and mix again. At first the Oats will feel wet, so let it stand for thirty seconds before mixing again. The texture that you are looking for is not slippery and wet to the touch, but a stiff mixture that does not ooze any liquid when you squeeze it tightly onto your weight. Let the ball of pack bait stand for a minute longer for the oats to further absorb the liquid before casting out.

The pack ball will partially break up on impact with the water, and continue to break apart around your hook bait once it has reached bottom. The oats and mashed fish particles will drift a scent trail into the current, leading your target fish back to your hook bait and chum pile.

About the Author

Throughout my adult life I am lucky enough to have travelled extensively for work purposes, and I have become expert in finding the space to pack a good quality travel rod into my bag. Among the fishing highlights on my travels, I have fished for big Stripers in the Colorado River below the Hoover Dam, jigged for Cod from the side of a lifeboat at Svalbard, and learned how to balloon fish over the reef, local style in Aruba.

If you see me fishing somewhere, stop and say hello, I am always happy to chat about the awesome shore fishing in Aruba.

Mike Harry